N[   ]ON

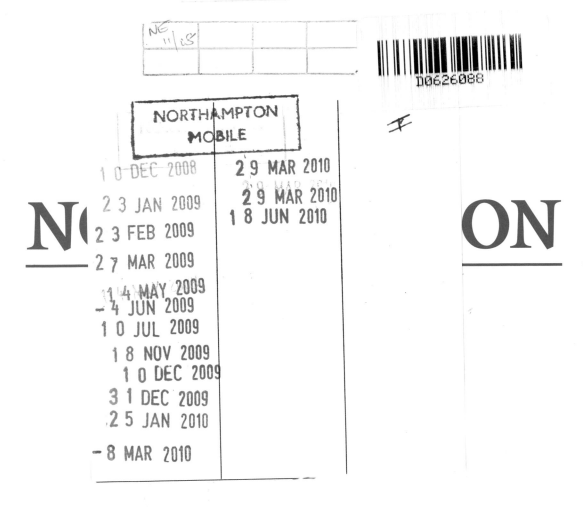

NORTHAMPTON
Chronicle
& ECHO

at heart ♡ publications

First Published in 2008 by:
At Heart Ltd,
32 Stamford Street, Altrincham,
Cheshire, WA14 1EY
in conjunction with
Northampton Chronicle & Echo,
Upper Mounts, Northampton, NN1 3HR

ISBN: 978-1-84547-186-6

Printed and bound by Bell & Bain Ltd, Glasgow

Northampton Geordie Club leaves for the North East in 1963 from outside the *Chronicle & Echo* on Northampton Market Square (see page 108).

Many of the pictures in this book would have been taken by the *Chron* photographers in this picture, taken at the paper's old premises in The Parade, Market Square, Northampton. From left are Roland Holloway, Cyril Arnold, Tony Smythe and Michael Walton with Suzy the corgi.

INTRODUCTION

Our first *Looking Back* book, produced in the summer of 2007, proved to be a local best-seller, with thousands flying off the shelves in Northamptonshire.

So, with around 30,000 photographs to choose from, it was not a difficult decision to go ahead with Volume Two!

As with the first book, this could not have been written without the help and enthusiasm of the *Chron's* readers, who have done the hard work by telling us just what was on the pictures we featured in the paper.

This reversal of the normal role of newspaper and reader – where you tell us what is going on - has proved to be one of the most popular features in the *Chron*. To recap for those new to *Looking Back*, in 2006 we took delivery of some 30,000 fragile glass negatives, the forerunner of photographic film, which had been exposed by the *Chron's* photographers, mainly in the 1950s and '60s but some much, much earlier.

The negatives, a unique record of news stories in Northamptonshire, had been stored in a county council warehouse in Guildhall Road, Northampton, since 1978. In 1996 this building caught fire but incredibly, although damage to the warehouse was great, firefighters managed to save the glass plates.

They languished in a backroom at Burton Latimer Library for nearly 10 years before the county council offered to return them to the *Chron*. Now they are back home and we use a few each week but, with the captions long-since disappeared, we rely on readers to provide the information.

Looking Back Volume Two is the result of that feedback and, as in Volume One, this book is dedicated to the *Chron's* loyal readers who made it possible.

AT WORK

● The female technician is the late Beryl Smith (née Plowman), says her sister Wendy Wilkins. She worked at Pettits, a leather dressing company in St Andrew's Road, Northampton, and tested dyes and other chemicals used in the leather industry. The photograph was taken between Beryl leaving Northampton School for Girls in 1951 and leaving the company to have her first child in 1956. Mrs Wilkins added that it was quite unusual at this time to find women working in scientific or industrial laboratories.
NBL2001

● The person handling the crate of chickens for Hudsons "The Game Men" of Northampton, is Tom Hope, says his cousin George Nutter. Tom worked for Hudsons most of his life.
NBL2002

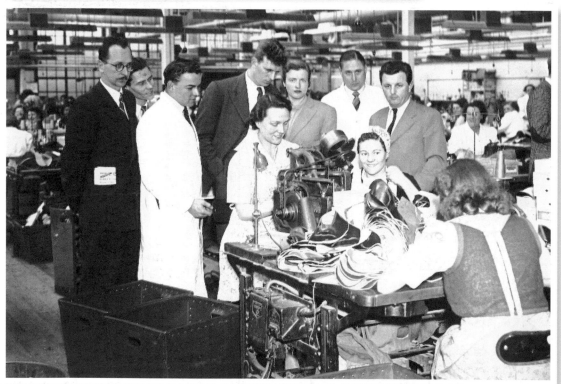

● This picture was taken in 1955 in the closing room of Barratt's factory, Northampton, says Jean Flaxman. The person in the white coat is her late husband Charles, who worked in the skin room as a leather buyer. He is seen showing around a group of Yugoslavian journalists. The lady on the eyeletting machine is Mrs G. Payne.
NBL2003

● Miss E. Harris tells us this is her father Mr F. Harris retiring after 50 years at the Central Ordnance Depot, Weedon, as store superintendent. Congratulating him is Lt Col G. Marshall, commanding officer at the depot. His retirement gifts are a barometer and an Anglepoise lamp.
NBL2004

● "The gentleman leaning on the fence is actually my pap, namely Walter Collier (1901-1979)," says Sheila Brockwell. "He was employed as a farm labourer by Richard Mackaness of Old Farm, Church Lane, Brafield-on-the-Green. The area where he is standing has recently been redeveloped and the outbuildings converted to stables and a livery yard."
NBL2005

● The porter at Ashby's auction rooms at Northampton is Frank Mockett, says his daughter Mrs S. Etheridge. Later he became a *Chronicle & Echo* vendor, standing at the old Derngate bus station and the County Ground.
NBL2006

● This is Councillor S. J. Ward operating his lathe, possibly in the 1930s, writes John Tomlinson. "He was a prolific and renowned model engineer. As well as being a member of Northampton Borough Council, he was a prominent member of Northampton Society of Model Engineers, which is still in existence and based at Lower Delapre Park, Northampton. Councillor Ward's obituary was published in Model Engineer in 1952. His largest model was that of a LMS railway crane which was on show at Euston Station for many years. This model, along with others, is now under the custodianship of The University of Northampton, the models actually belonging to Northamptonshire County Council. One railway model was purchased by a society member who still runs it on the track at Lower Delapre Park. On his death, the lathe was bequeathed to Northampton Society of Model Engineers who had it set up in basement rooms at Thornton Hall. When the Society constructed its meeting room at Lower Delapre Park in the mid-1980s, I purchased the lathe as my entry into model engineering. As I progressed, I purchased a more modern lathe and sold the old lathe at Holcot Steam Rally auction."

NBL2007

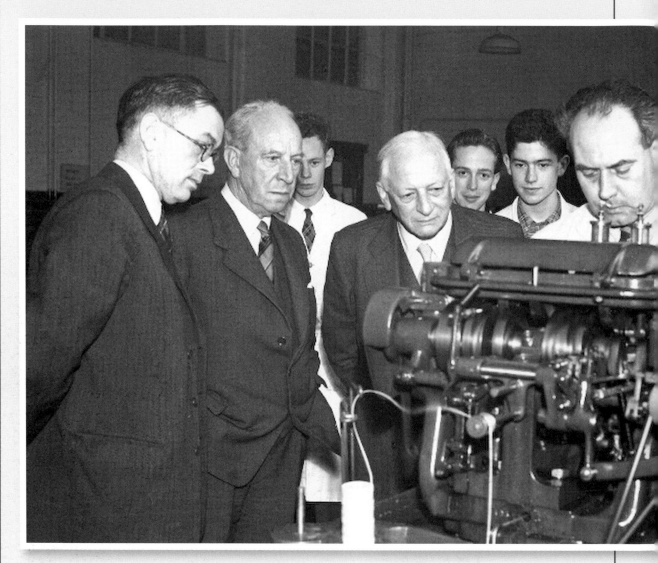

● Samuel Allen writes: "This is a picture of the former boot and shoe department in the College of Technology in St George's Avenue, Northampton, now known as The University of Northampton, Avenue Campus. The person wearing glasses is John Thornton, head of the department, standing alongside the principal, Oliver Bailey, looking at Harry Steel, a lecturer in the making department in the white coat operating a Model O stitcher. The photograph was taken sometime between 1951 and 1955." A. W. Adams also recognised Mr Bailey from the picture.
NBL2008

● Sometimes we take a guess at what is on a mystery glass negative and sometimes we get it wrong! These wooden boxes which we at first thought were coffins turned out to be large organ pipes. Eric Cave told us: "It would appear that the pipes form part of the pedal organ, 32 feet open diapason stop, from a large organ. It is possible that the photograph shows the manufacture of pipes for the 1895 Walker organ in St Matthew's Church, Northampton. This organ has recently undergone a major restoration by Harrisons of Durham in association with local organ builder Kenneth Tickell." Gervase Forsyth adds: "There was an organ manufacturer in Campbell Square, Northampton, Davis Organ Co." Mr Tickell confirmed they were wooden organ pipes but thought it likely that the ones for St Matthew's would have been made at Walker's workshops at Ruislip. NBL2009

● The two gentlemen are Harry Smith (left) and Harold Pickard at Midland Carpet Company in Sheep Street, Northampton, says Jenny Cotter. "I think it was taken in 1962 or '63 when I was a teenager and worked in my uncle's sweet and tobacco shop where the two mentioned above, Mr Kirby their manager and Robin Clark, their gorgeous junior, used to shop."
NBL2010

● John Smith says this is him repairing the track at Piddington Station after a fire in 1958 or '59. From left to right are Raymond, Mr Smith, Bert Underwood and Frank Freeman. Mr Smith is the only surviving member of the gang and added that Piddington Station was nearer Horton than Piddington.
NBL2011

● Michael Gardner tells us that the doors to All Saints Church, Northampton, were being worked on in 1967 by the Bonsor and Wilding joinery firm. "I was 18 then and helped load the doors onto a lorry. A complete set of doors and frames was made from oak in the workshops by skilled craftsmen." Mr Gardner was able to name Bill Pearson, Terry Broughton, Fred Birch, Peter Davies and Bob Alderman.
NBL2012

● The man on the left with the television detector van is Walter Tompkins, writes his nephew Kenneth Beeden. "Apart from his war service in the RAF, he spent all his working life with the Post Office, mainly based at St Giles Street. He was awarded an Imperial Service Medal in recognition of his long service." The other man is Albert Charles Homer, says his son B. C. Homer.
NBL2013

● Mrs B. Vanags recognised her late husband John spraying a car at Duston Coachworks in the late 1960s. Michael Bell added: "John was a very good local table tennis player who was born in Poland and came to England where he married and settled down. Sadly John passed away many years ago." And Susan Dauksta recognised her late brother-in-law. She writes: "John worked for my husband Vladislavs (commonly known as Charles) who was the founder of Duston Coachworks. John was born in Riga, Latvia, and was a loved and respected friend and countryman of my husband. He came to this country as a displaced person in 1947. My husband retired 11 years ago at the age of 72 when the business was sold."
NBL2014

● Both these employees at Jones and Sons shoe shop in St Giles Street, Northampton, around 1966, have been named by Mrs B. Joyce. Left is June Millard, the manageress, and she is with Anne Joyce, Mrs Joyce's daughter.
NBL2015

● "The lady in the photo is Mrs Barbara Whyatt who worked at A. Bell and Co in Gold Street, Northampton, around 40 years ago, writes Mrs M. Hunt. She added that Bell's showrooms were now in Kingsthorpe.
NBL2016

● A former newspaper colleague emails: "I am the Richard Field referred to in your story and fascinated to see pictures taken around the time when I become editor of the *Mercury & Herald* in 1965. The man is holding a copy of the *Mercury & Herald* (which I redesigned) but I can't identify him, although I suspect he is an American. His suit looks like one of American lightweight design. I did escort a group of Northampton people to Northampton, Massachusetts, in 1964 and this picture may be connected with that visit. Later, in 1970, I was at the helm when the *Mercury* reached its 250th anniversary, and we had the Duchess of Gloucester attend our big celebration at the Town Hall (maybe the subject of some future pictures you may unearth). Copies of the 250th anniversary colour supplement (something unique at the time) are still around. After leaving Northampton in 1972 I worked in newspapers throughout the group, with periods at Wigan, Preston, Sheffield and Leeds, until my retirement in 2002. I now live in North Yorkshire and keep my hand in by editing a website for the village where I live. By the way, Ken Nutt, my former deputy editor, still lives in Northampton."

"Another point which may be of interest. My mother ("Auntie Dick") ran the Merry Comrades, a children's circle, in that paper for over 40 years and during that time raised large sums of money for local hospitals, etc. Her story is told in *Ladies of Distinction in Northamptonshire* by Mia Butler and Colin Eaton (published in 2005). Your current project in archiving 30,000 glass negatives is an excellent one. I suspect a good many of them have been taken by photographers Roland Holloway, Bob Price and Alan Burman, all colleagues and friends of mine at the time."

NBL2017

● David Phipps says he vividly recalls the mid-1960s incident which led to these overhead wires being repaired. He writes: "It happened on the loop line to Northampton down the sidings shunting yard, opposite Northampton number four signal box.
The men on the ladders are repairing the overhead electric cables after the derailment of several fuel-carrying tankers, some of which ended on their side. These were destined for the Esso petroleum depot close to Kingsthorpe Mill Lane railway bridge. The down sidings marshalling yard runs parallel to the rear of houses in Pembroke Road, Spencer. I was head shunter at the Northampton up sidings to the rear of number four signal box."
NBL2018

● The men working on All Saints Church, Northampton, are Harry Pulny and Mick Bakai, says George Ward. "They were Ukrainians employed by SGB Ltd as I was. The photo was taken about 1959-60. They were first-class scaffolders and decent men."
NBL2019

● "The steelwork being erected here is for the new entrance, offices and hall of the College of Technology, St George's Avenue, Northampton," writes Geoff Forsyth. "I believe it was around 1960 as I was a part-time student there at the time. This is now of course The University of Northampton."
NBL2020

Pioneer Surgeon

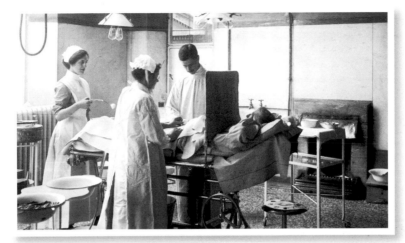

● Memories were reawakened for a former patient of a Northampton General Hospital surgeon when she saw his photograph in the *Chronicle & Echo* more than 80 years after he treated her.

Dr Charles Holman was the first orthopaedic surgeon at Northampton General Hospital where he worked from 1912 until his retirement in 1952. Betty Martin was a little girl when she was treated by Dr Holman for a calcium deficiency and she has very fond memories of him.

The 88-year-old from Kingsthorpe, Northampton, told us: "I was born in 1918 and I saw him before I was school age. I had to have irons in my leg to keep my legs straight. I remember that he used to put me on his knee and say 'it's my little sweetheart'. He would give me an apple and an orange. When I saw the photograph in the paper, it brought back memories. I was looked after by my grandmother and she used to say he was a lovely man and he was one of the best doctors down there."

This rare photograph is thought to date back to around the time of World War One. The hospital's archivist, Sue Longworth, said it was a fascinating find and a good representation of how procedures were carried out at the beginning of the 20th century. She added: "During his 40 years in the town, Charles Colgate Holman set up an orthopaedic outpatient unit, carried out ear, nose and throat procedures and was the sole operating obstetrician in the district for many years."

Dr Holman also started a fracture clinic in the hospital and supervised this until the appointment of the orthopaedic surgeons after the war.

He strove to raise the level of care at the hospital and pressed for the appointment of specialised doctors.

In the book *A History of Northampton General Hospital*, by Dr F. Waddy, it said: "Holman was rather shy and quite incapable of forwarding his own interests or advertising himself. He was a highly-skilled surgeon, whose results were as good as any and better than most surgeons in the country."

"The Northampton General Hospital owes a great debt to Holman, who did so much unselfish work in its development."

Charles Holman died in June 1954.

NBL2021

DRAMA AND THE ARTS

● The mystery of this sign advertising The New Palace of Varieties has been cleared up by readers. According to the website www.northampton.org.uk, the Palace of Varieties opened in 1901 at the bottom of Gold Street, Northampton. The sign notes the theatre had a "Good array of talent. Change of programme each week. Popular prices."

The enamel advertising sign was blue with white lettering, Tony Perrett told us. He adds: "I have one, there is one in Abington Park Museum and I know of at least one other. The Palace of Varieties was on the corner at the junction of Gold Street and Horseshoe Street." Sue Edwards also has one of the signs, which she bought from an antiques shop in Kettering Road, Northampton.

Lisa Cottrell comments: "The shop in the photograph belonged to my grandfather, William Christopher Cross. It was in Wellingborough Road, quite close to Abington Square. He was a bespoke shoemaker. The picture must have been taken between 1946-60. My mother has no idea why the sign was above the shop. It is interesting for us, particularly as I have worked in the theatre profession for 30 years. Maybe it was a 'sign'!"

NBL2022

● Winifred Bradbury was delighted to see a picture of her late father, William Aistrope, looking at a bust of Shakespeare in the foyer of the Royal Theatre in the 1950s. She says: "My dad attended a Shakespeare play as a guest of the *Chronicle & Echo* because he had written a couple of scathing letters to you about the amount of time devoted to Shakespeare on the television. I still have the cuttings from the dear old *Chron*."
NBL2023

● Rosalind Gibson writes: "Yes, it's me being made-up by Miss Margaret Gillingham. It was 1955 and the play was Charles Kingsley's *Water Babies*, being performed by our class of Weston Favell C of E School in the Schools' Drama Festival held at Moulton Secondary Modern School. Others in the picture are Barbara Maycock, Susan Pinches, Linda Dyer and Richard Seaby (I think!). They were certainly some of the happiest days of my life, under the headship of Harry Hawkins, his wife Gladys and Robert Crook."
NBL2024

● Maureen Dunkley (née Bromage) not only recognised herself in this picture of Northampton Amateur Operatic Company's cast of *The Quaker Girl*, but also sent us the original cutting from March 11, 1960. She is circled and says the man in the centre is Richard Rogers. The opera was performed at the Savoy Cinema, now the Jesus Centre, in Abington Square. Trevor Bailey says the rehearsal was taking place at the St George's Girls School and was able to name Maisie Griffith, Susan Farr, Derek Needle, Pete Griffith, Les Wilmur, Terry Curzon, Joyce Hodgekiss, Pat Peach and Brian Hall.

NBL2025

NBL2026

● When we used these pictures in the *Chron's* Looking Back feature, we guessed that they were of a performance of Gilbert and Sullivan's *HMS Pinafore* and we were correct. Mark Gibson writes: "These were taken at the former Northampton Town and County Grammar School for Boys in Billing Road [now NSB] in December 1955. The part of the First Lord of the Admiralty was played by Mr E. B. Johnson, who taught Latin. Able Seaman Dick Deadeye was played by Mr Jack Searle, who taught geography and later went on to be headteacher at Towcester. Young "ladies" may include Bob Brown, David Peet and Stephen Meakins. These performances gave those of us who took part a wonderful grounding in singing and music in general and a number of my contemporaries became well-respected professional musicians."

NBL2027

● Retired journalist Ken Nutt writes: "This shows my parents, Councillor and Mrs George Nutt, then Mayor and Mayoress of Northampton, and, on the left, Councillor John Poole, chairman of Northampton Museums and Libraries Committee. The occasion was the opening of the Art Alive exhibition in the Art Gallery, Guildhall Road, in 1960."
NBL2028

● This was taken at Northampton's Salon Ballroom on the occasion of the United Commercial Travellers' Association "Big Night Out", writes Ken Brown, who is pictured talking to top ventriloquist Arthur Worsley and his doll Charlie Brown. Mr Brown was chairman of the association. Chairman of the Northampton branch of the association, Ken Andrews, reckoned the picture was taken in the late 1960s or early '70s. Keith Loynes commented that Arthur Worsley was *the* ventriloquist of his day.
NBL2029

● Lots of readers wrote to tell us this is a young Peter Newcombe, a former Towcester Grammar School pupil and a now an artist of some repute, hanging his work with Tom Osborne Robinson, scenic designer of the Royal Theatre, Northampton. The year was 1968 and the occasion was an exhibition of Mr Newcombe's drawings entitled *Homage to Clare* at Northampton Museum and Art Gallery to celebrate the 175th anniversary of poet John Clare. Thanks to Anthony Ward, Diana Hibbert, C. Wilcox, Estelle Rose and others for supplying the information.

NBL2030

● The violinist is Alfredo Campoli (1906-91) who made several appearances in Northampton, write Anthony Ward and R. Penn. Neither could name the woman with him. Campoli was pictured backstage at the now-demolished New Theatre where Alfred Marks was starring in *Spring and Port Wine*.

NBL2031

● This is Philip Berrill hanging his own artwork at a local exhibition in the 1960s, helped by Christina Moore, who emails: "You covered many of the events of TANGENT, which blossomed out of the highly respected Northampton School of Art. The main body of TANGENT comprised myself, Brian Dunstone and the late Malcolm Pollard, with some valued input from fellow student Roger Wilkin." Christina remembered students, including herself, making a giant fish for the annual Art School Revel. She adds: "It blew away from the top of the Salon roof soon after the event!"
NBL2032

● The piano player was the star of *Coronation Street,* Dennis Tanner, and he was at Litchborough Youth Club probably in about 1964, says Sylvia Mold. "In the photo was Colleen Walker, Rosemary and Francis Manning, Janet Hakin, Malcolm Etheridge, the Boreham family, Robert and Howard Corn, myself, Angela Floyd and Jean Nightingale. Sitting on his knee was Patsy Piper." An internet search reveals that Philip Lowrie played Elsie Tanner's son Dennis, who was the first "bad boy" of the street.
NBL2033

● This is the Tony Cockerill Band, and Tony himself writes: "We were rehearsing for a gig at the Salon-de-Danse, Franklin's Gardens, for the Northampton College of Technology Students' Union in, I think, 1957. I continued with my own band at university but then I forsook musical notes to study the financial ones. I became an economics lecturer, teaching at Cambridge, Lancaster and Durham universities. Last year I returned to Cambridge as Leverhulme Professor of Economics."

All but two of the band were named by Alan Hollowell. He writes: "Front line, left to right, are trumpet Tony Barratt, son of the Musicians' Union secretary Charlie Barratt, on alto sax Johnny Harris, who is still going strong today with his own Johnny Harris Big Band and very well known to Northamptonians, then Ray Robinson, also on alto sax and myself on tenor sax. Ray and myself spent many years as regular members of the Jimmy Wooding Band. The room we are rehearsing in is at the rear of the Black Lion (now Wig and Pen) in St Giles Street, Northampton. Both Ray and I have original copies of the photograph." The other two musicians are Don Clarke (bass) and Geoff Locke (drums).
NBL2034

● Vera Marshall was able to tell us that this is the Northampton Rehearsal Dance Orchestra. She says: "The musicians used to meet once a week to play the music of the big bands in the lounge of the Hare and Hounds in Newland, Northampton, courtesy of the landlord Peter Williamson. I believe this picture was taken when they were augmented by some professional players of well-known dance bands of the day. I was so happy to see the picture because my late husband Ron Marshall was in it. He is the trombone player on the far right and Tom Thorneycroft was the trombonist next-but-one to him. Thank you for printing this picture. It made my day!"

NBL2035

● "This is young Steven O'Connor who lived in Merthyr Road, Northampton," says Jean Lillis. "He was my son's friend and a very talented young man. I believe he still lives in Kings Heath. It was taken about 1960-2 and I remember the great excitement when his picture and write-up appeared in the *Chron*." NBL2036

● The Saxon Skiffle Group used to play at various places in Northampton, including upstairs at the Kettering Road Co-op, writes Mrs B. Bromwich. "My husband Dave is second left playing the guitar before doing his National Service. His brother Neville is second from right at the back." Note that the bass player has improvised with a broom handle and a tea chest! NBL2037

NBL2038

NBL2039

● This Salvation Army group were called the Joy Strings, several readers told us. "They got into the charts in the 1960s," emails Phil Boswell. "The woman on the left in the group picture was Joy Webb, who was as near to a leader as the Joystrings had. The group came to Northampton in the summer of 1964 and played at the Drill Hall in Clare Street to a packed audience. Before the concert, one of the bass guitarist's strings broke and the day was saved by local Army member Barrie Willis who gave one of the strings of his bass that he had brought with him to the concert."

Mrs C. Roe added that one of the men was Peter Dalziel. Sue Edwards also recognised Joy Webb. "In the 1960s she and her group became very well known and were on television quite a lot. Joy wrote her own music. I really enjoy this series and often see people I know."

Finally, retired Salvation Army officer Gordon Sharp adds: "For about 18 months in 1965-7, I was the 'roadie' for the group and was happy to accompany them to my home town. The group's repertoire was certainly a departure from the rather staid image of the Army at that time. Joy Webb was awarded the highest internal honour with the Army and is living in retirement in London. Peter Dalziel and Sylvia Gair (to the right of the picture) subsequently married and spent a lifetime in service as Salvation Army officers. Wycliffe Noble (centre back), the drummer, was the only lay member of the group. The other member was Bill Davidson."

● Lots of readers named the talented Will Yeomans as the piano player but only one was able to recognise Harold Nash standing at his side.

Anna Ruzicka emails: "Harold Nash lived at 36 Bostock Avenue, Northampton, for more than 50 years. He was an organist and one of his jobs was playing the rising organ for silent films in the cinema. He and his wife Nella spent all their lives with music and acting and both were active members of the Gilbert and Sullivan Society here. They both taught music and had a wide circle of pupils and friends. We are sure there are quite a few people in Northampton who still remember them."

Mark Gibson thought the picture was taken in the late 1960s. He adds: "Will was a gifted pianist. He was an eminent musicologist with a vast collection of musical instruments, some of which can be seen hanging on the wall behind him. He used to take his collection around the country and frequently gave lectures. He was also an inspirational teacher and I studied piano with him for a number of years. During the time I was having piano lessons, Will was building his own harpsichord. Some time in the 1970s, I think, Will and his wife Elizabeth moved away from Northampton."

Anthony Ward attended musical appreciation classes at Will's spacious home in Billing Road from 1968-73. He adds: "He had the second oldest piano in the country and we were politely but firmly asked not to put our tea cups on its ancient surface. Will was an exceptionally courteous man and dressed as an early Victorian with flowing white hair, bow tie, long jacket, waistcoat and fob watch."

Retired journalist Ken Nutt knew Bill Yeomans well and was in the same class at school. *Chron* columnist Eric Roberts recalled: "Will's main interest was the harpsichord on which he held the record for playing an incredible number of notes in one minute. I took Will and his harpsichord to Birmingham to feature this accomplishment on television. I lost touch with him and his wife Elizabeth when they moved to Wales although we continued to exchange Christmas cards."

Other information on this remarkable man came from Geoff Astle and Trevor Bailey.
NBL2040

IN UNIFORM

● "This is our dad, Dick Francis, Traffic Warden number 12," write sisters Jennifer Gleeson and Linda Skippen. "It was so lovely to see him in his uniform . . . he was so proud of his job. We don't know why he was being interviewed by the *Chron* in the Market Square."
NBL2041

● Helen Allen recognised her late husband Supt A. V. Allen on parade with other offices of Northamptonshire Police. He is on the far right. "Next to him is the late Chief Superintendent George Swain. The tall officer facing the camera is the late Chief Constable John Gott. The photograph was taken at Wootton Hall during the 1960s."
NBL2042

● The lady presenting the cake at Northampton General Hospital children's ward is June Berwick, now Mrs Huntley, who writes: "Also in the picture is Janet Mann and my brother Brian (second from right). The occasion was an anniversary of the ABC Cinema Minors Saturday morning club. Janet and I were original members and my brother a current member. The picture was taken around 1960." Susan Hassett (née Adams) adds: "I am the little girl in the corner. The ABC Minors held a birthday card competition and I won. I was asked to go with some of the cinema staff to the hospital to present the birthday cake." Sheila Woodhouse writes: "The staff nurse is my friend Margaret Loveys, who died quite young after devoting years to caring for premature babies at the Barratt Maternity Home."
NBL2043

● Ian Clark recognised the premises of Stimpson and Perkins Leather Tannery at Abington Mills in Northampton. He says: "The premises stood on farmland then owned by Farmer Wilson for many years and was recently demolished following arson attacks in previous years. My father Alf Clark worked there during the war years and retired after 40 years of service to the company. My brother and myself were also employed there for many years until sadly the company closed in the late 1970s and became abandoned and in a bad state of repair. Several fires occurred at the premises throughout its history and one is depicted in the photo but this looks like it was around the late 1950s era. Sadly its demise ended in the late '90s when alleged arsonists finally caused it to be demolished to make way for new housing. It holds a lot of memories for my family." Ron Cripps reckons the fire brigade may have just been filling up their tenders from the river.

NBL2044

● An extraordinary amount of information on this picture comes from Northampton aircraft historian Robert Allen of the Twinwood Aviation Museum. He says: "The photograph was taken on November 1, 1960, and shows fireman spraying foam on the crater containing the burning remains of an American Air Force RB66 Destroyer, a photo-reconnaissance aircraft attached to the 1st Tactical Reconnaissance Squadron, 10th Tactical Reconnaissance Wing at RAF Alconbury, Hunts. The aircraft was on a training flight when there was an in-flight power failure and one of the aircraft's engines completely cut out. The crew of three had no option but to eject from the crippled aircraft which flew on un-manned for two miles and crashed into the crown of Bulls Hill, missing Bulls Hill farm by 200 yards. The crater can still be seen today close to the old ruined Dower House in Fawsley Park, near Badby. The three American crew members bailed out safely and were pilot 1st Lieutenant Larry Fealy, navigator 1st Lieutenant Peter J. Hollitscher and engineer Staff Sergeant J. R. Gaskill."
NBL2045

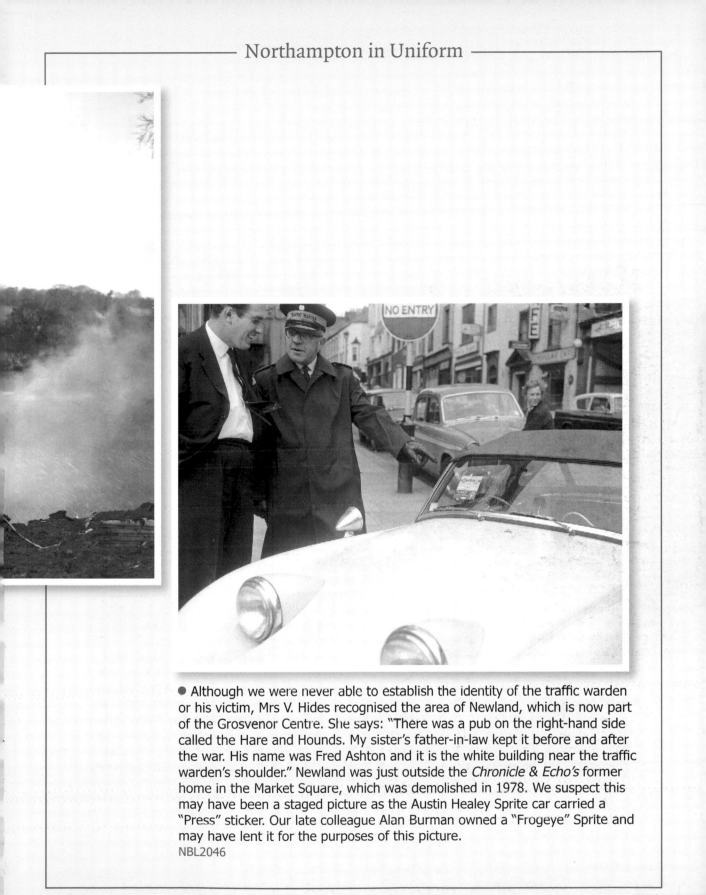

● Although we were never able to establish the identity of the traffic warden or his victim, Mrs V. Hides recognised the area of Newland, which is now part of the Grosvenor Centre. She says: "There was a pub on the right-hand side called the Hare and Hounds. My sister's father-in-law kept it before and after the war. His name was Fred Ashton and it is the white building near the traffic warden's shoulder." Newland was just outside the *Chronicle & Echo's* former home in the Market Square, which was demolished in 1978. We suspect this may have been a staged picture as the Austin Healey Sprite car carried a "Press" sticker. Our late colleague Alan Burman owned a "Frogeye" Sprite and may have lent it for the purposes of this picture.

NBL2046

● "The lady seated on the right is Miss Mary Coombe, Matron at Northampton General Hospital," says Tony Perrett. "The gentleman with the bow tie is Fred Pragnell who was a ward orderly on Compton Ward, which would suggest that the presentation is for one of the staff from that ward."
NBL2047

● Anne Tysoe (née Thatcher) tells us she is the middle nurse holding a Christmas or New Year baby at the Barratt Maternity Home, Northampton. Her fellow SRNs fifty or so years ago were Pam Allard (left) and Dympna Bailey.
NBL2048

● This is the 24th Abington Church (St Peter's and Paul's) Cub Scouts Pack outside the parish rooms at the corner of Park Avenue North and Ashburnham Road, Northampton, says Flight Lieutenant Phil Andrews BEM. He says: "We were heading off, I think, to Scout Jamboree at Gilwell Park in 1968. The picture may have been taken by Cyril Harte, *Chron* journalist, whose son Patrick was in the Cub pack. I am squatting second left front row. I was called Tiny Andrews as I was the younger brother of Paul Andrews, who died of a brain tumour when only 22. Others in the picture are Scout leader Bob Garrett with his fiancée Glynis, Bill Parsonson, Akela (Cub leader) Mrs Scott, her son Gavin, Colin Hetherington (his brother Dave was a Scout, and father Dennis our Quartermaster), one of the Nicklin brothers and Steve Pendred. We were a very jolly scouting group, the success due to family atmosphere with numerous brothers and sisters in Scouts, Cubs, Guides and Brownies, with parents helping the fantastic leaders along the way. We had father and son camps, Scout and Guide parties and a Pathfinder youth club too. I spent three to four nights a week with this scouting family, learning life skills. Whole families in the Abington area were involved: Andrews, Malpas, Hetherington, Nicklin, Jarman, Johnson, Roderick, Wilkinson, Thacker, Lack, Heathman, Fitzgibbons, Heathcote, and many more. In the early '70s Scout Troops pushed all their equipment (tents, camping stoves and food) on wooden carts to Overstone camp site. We raised funds through jumble sales and collecting in local streets. One night we knocked on a door around tea-time and were asked to wait. We were then handed a glass crystal serving bowl with the remnants of some jelly. We were too shocked to say anything! Around 1970, 24th Abington Scouts won the Thornton Trophy, the town Scout camping competition at Overstone camp site and were runners-up around 1973.

NBL2049

● "This was taken at the Royal Pioneer Corps Depot, Simpson Barracks, Wootton, outside the HQ building in the early 1960s, probably 1963," says Colonel John Royle. "The man in the centre is Lt Col Edward Archer MBE, Commandant of the Royal Pioneer Corps Depot with, on the right of the picture, his Second-in-Command, Major John Logan. The man on the left is the Director of Army Pioneers and Labour, a brigadier whose name I cannot recall. However, I believe I can identify the Triumph as a TR2, already past its prime, which belonged to the education officer of the unit. The car might appear smart in the picture, but was extremely scruffy inside and always seemed to be occupied by a small dog."
NBL2050

● The young lady receiving her Queen's Guide Award in 1966 is Pamela Smith of the 19th Northampton (St Giles) Guides. Pamela Wood writes: "The presentation is being made by Mrs Dennis (who later became Mrs Richards), the County Commissioner. The Guider in the centre is Joan Walden, Captain of St Giles Guides."
NBL2051

● Graham Martin used to work for Northampton Caravans Ltd and helped build this special unit for the St John Ambulance Brigade's Kingsthorpe Divisions. In the picture are Mr R. W. Smith of the St John and Mr C. Whatton, manager of Northampton Caravans. The caravan was paid for by Northampton and District Working Men's Clubs and dedicated by the Bishop of Peterborough in May 1967.
NBL2052

● Regular Looking Back informant Tony Perrett tells us: "The five nurses facing the camera have been identified by my sister, Carole Perrett, who although not shown herself, was in the same year-group. Carole thinks that it is from 1964 or 1965. The nurses are, from left to right, Dolores Quinn, Anne Cummings, Jennifer Digby, Lyn Drage and Sue Rudd." Kathryn Roberts recognised her mother Joy Roberts in the picture which she says was taken in 1964 at the prize-giving graduation. Lyn Frost (née Drage) spotted herself but had a different recollection of the names. She writes: "Third from left is Joy Groom and far right is Gillian Sibley. I am between Joy and Gill. We trained together and were great friends."
NBL2053

● Mr T. N. Parker tells us that this is Mrs Tate, the post lady for Piddington and part of Hackleton, pictured in the 1960s.
NBL2054

Making of the M1 Motorway

This series of pictures was in a box marked "New road, 58, Rothersthorpe and Collingtree and Shell-Mex/Newport Pagnell". It shows the building of the M1 motorway, the first section of which opened in November 1959.

● The scene at Collingtree on March 22, 1958. Note the helicopter landing pad marked out with a large "H". Engineers kept an eye on the huge project by flying up and down the route of the M1 in a Bell 47 helicopter.
NBL2055

● The tanker filling up, probably at Newport Pagnell, was pictured on April 3, 1958.
NBL2056

NBL2057

● These two photographs were taken at Collingtree on March 24, 1958.

NBL2058

NBL2059

● Children at Rothersthorpe are taking advantage of the roadworks by collecting firewood and transporting it on a home-made trolley.

NBL2060

SPORT

● Lots of readers recognised members of Northampton Weightlifting Club in 1954-5, and in particular Keith Pickering, who is lifting the weights (below). Former members Albert Dann, Frank Holmes, Don Bates and Paul Desborough are all on the group picture and wrote to us with information. The club met in a cellar under the church rooms in Regent Square. Others on the picture are Mac Fulton, P. Brockhall, Frank Warren and Ken Bailey.

NBL2061

NBL2062

● This is Monks Park Bowls Club with the Crockett Cup, agree Mrs N. Andrews, whose father Mr H. Vaughan is standing second from right, and Mrs Knight, whose father is also in the picture. Mr E. Smith, president of Abington Park Bowls League, confirmed the picture was taken in the park and added that the magnificent trophy was still being competed for.
NBL2063

● Emily Twiselton is pictured here in February 1958. She writes: "Daphne Laverick and I went on to win the ladies' doubles cup at the Northampton Table Tennis league final. The cups were presented by Mr W. Cowper Barrons, league president and editor of the *Chronicle & Echo*. I am still playing, but not in the league. I always look out for the pictures from the past and my husband has recognised some of the pictures but I didn't expect to see myself."
NBL2064

● The start of this cycle race was near the church in Abington Park, Northampton, in the mid-1960s, says A. D. Hiam. "The different hooped shirts indicate the different teams and clubs involved in a 15-25 mile round trip. I'm guessing those in the front belonged to Northampton Wheelers Cycle Club." Brian Paling adds that the group was headed by local riders Ian Reid and the late Roy Cottingham.

NBL2065

● This is the Bradford and Bingley Building Society golf team in the late 1960s or early '70s, say Malcolm Pounds and Mrs H. Clarke. From left are Geoffrey Johnson, Mr Pounds, Gordon Lodge and David Barber. Mr Pounds says they were taking part in the *Chronicle & Echo* team competition at Kingsthorpe Golf Club. He thinks his team lost in the final to Old Wellingburians.

NBL2066

● The man with the dragster is Mark Stratton, of Fosters Booth, says Ray Darlow, who used to help him build the cars. The car shown had a Chevrolet engine and the body of a BSA car, which caused a controversy at the time, as they were very rare. The car in the background is a 1955 or '56 Chevrolet. Mr Stratton's sister-in-law Mrs J Dunkley added that Mark died 14 years ago.
NBL2067

● Jill Snedker recognised two old friends, sadly no longer alive. "On the right is Violet Chamberlain, an excellent golfer, hockey player and coach of the English team, and on the left Hilda Castell, her regular partner from Wellingborough Golf Club."
NBL2068

● "This is from the 1960s when the Towcestrians Rugby Football and Cricket Club held an annual tug-o'-war across the River Tove for charity," emails Frank Jeffs. "The Men's Own RFC always entered a team just for fun and to support the charity. They wanted to get in the river early, make a splash then get showered ready for an early pint at the clubhouse. The person just getting out with his hands on the bank is yours truly and the person behind me is John Ashby who has sadly now passed on. The Men's Own RFC went on to take part in many Northampton Carnivals and raised good contributions for the charities."
NBL2069

● Lots of information on this old Cobblers picture comes from Martin Kennedy. He writes: "This was taken at Oxford United prior to a pre-season friendly in 1963-4 season. The players are, back row: Terry Branston, Chic Brodie, Joe Kiernan, Frank Large, Derek Leck and Tony Claypole. Front row: Billy Hails, Ray Smith, John Reid, Barry Lines and Mike Everitt. This was the first game where the Cobblers wore the club badge on their shirts. Joe Kiernan was voted as the Cobblers all-time legend by your readers and this game was his first for the club. In the previous season the club had won Division Three. In 1965 they were in Division One with four players from this team picture – Branston, Leck, Lines and Everitt – having played in all four divisions... a feat no-one else had ever achieved before."
NBL2070

● This is Barry Stock with a 21 3/4 lb pike at Ironstone Quarry, Northampton Road, Towcester, on October 3, 1963, say his parents.
NBL2071

● Phyllis Stafford recognised Towcester Racecourse and says the man on the right is Major John Schillizi and with his back to camera is leading trainer Fred Winter. The weighing room is in the background, she adds.
NBL2072

● Local hunts have provided information about two of our old pictures. Phillippa White emails: "This is Joe Miller, huntsman of the Grafton hounds for 20 years from 1953 to 1972. He died quite recently having spent his retirement in Paulerspury. It is obviously taken in Towcester and we had our Boxing Day meets there until quite recently."
NBL2073

● Jason Gordon of the Oakley Hunt emails: "The picture shows huntsman Stanley Hardiman at the old kennels in Milton Ernest, Bedfordshire, with his hounds. The pictures would have been taken in about 1959-60. Stanley Hardiman was huntsman for the Oakley from 1951 until he retired due to ill health in 1965."
NBL2074

● Cricket broadcaster and historian Andrew Radd was able to confirm this was taken during the Northamptonshire v New Zealand match in August 1958. He emails: "It was a rain-affected draw... it was a very wet summer. The only real highlight was a century by the Kiwis' star man John Reid. The picture shows county skipper Raman Subba Row leading out the side, followed by senior pro Dennis Brookes and Des Barrick."
NBL2075

● This is a cricket match on Northampton Racecourse between Avon Cosmetics and Roade, says Terry Lyons. The Avon players are Arthur Collins (captain), Bill Behan, Terry himself (who played for both clubs) and Trevor Harrison. Roade players are Doug Walker (captain) and Frank Johnson. Dennis Hoare adds: "I recognise the captain in the white sweater as Arthur Collins."
NBL2076

TRANSPORT

● Lots of readers recognised the showrooms of Shale and Woodrow in Cliftonville, Northampton, pictured in around 1963. The Austin A40 shown was obviously the latest model.
NBL2077

● David Barry recognised himself as the mechanic working on the Lambretta. He was employed by Norman Stokes in Vernon Street, Northampton.
NBL2078

● The gentleman is riding past Campbell Square School into Campbell Street, Northampton. "Actually," writes Eddie Rowe, "he is a very old friend of mine, Andre Baldet, on one of his motorcycles. He was later well known as 'Motobaldet' through his chain of garages in and around Northampton during the 1960s, '70s and '80s and his connection with scooters and motorcycle sport. I believe his business started in the 1950s selling mopeds and scooters from a shop at the corner of Newland and Princes Street near the old Temperance Hall Cinema. Tony Perrett agreed it was Mr Baldet, who died in March 2008.
NBL2079

● The late, legendary Northampton businessman Andre Baldet is again pictured, this time with his dual-control Vespa scooter in the yard of the fire station, Campbell Square, Northampton. Another set of handlebars enabled an experienced rider to control the machine while the learner sat in front!
NBL2080

● "The man on the telephone inside the Heron at Sywell Aerodrome was Raymond Way, owner of Shackleton Aviation, based at Sywell in the 1960s," writes B. E. Minards, managing director of the aerodrome from 1983-93. He adds: "After the photograph was taken, I joined Mr Way on a flight from Sywell to Leavesden Aerodrome, near Watford."
NBL2081

VISITING AIRCRAFT PARK

HACKLETON'S

● Ben Brown, secretary of Sywell Aviation Museum, has confirmed that this De Havilland DH 114 Heron was pictured at the aerodrome and he thinks it was around 1963-4. With the help of the internet he was able to tell us that Heron G-ASFI had a busy and varied career after being built in the mid-1950s. In 1957 the aircraft was acquired by the Luftwaffe, and its passengers included German Chancellor Konrad Adenauer. In 1963 it was re-registered as G-ASFI by Shackleton Aviation of Sywell and the next year went overseas. The Heron turned up in 1970 in Alice Springs, Northern Territory, Australia. It flew for various small airlines in Australia and Fiji until 2003, when it was acquired by the Australian Aviation Museum, Bankstown, New South Wales, Australia, where it still resides. Its owner told us it was awaiting restoration.
NBL2082

● "The photograph of the railway carriage inside a factory is from the early 1960s," writes George Gibbins. "It was one of three occasions, I believe, when trains were accidentally shunted into the fabrication shop at A. H. Allen on the corner of Gladstone Road and Spencer Bridge. The sidings ran at the back of houses in Gladstone Road and Pembroke Road and if the train was long, due to the curve, the train driver could not see the other end of the train. I think on two occasions coaches were pushed in and once it was a loaded goods wagon. Miraculously, despite the presence of quite a few workers each time, no-one was ever injured. I was an apprentice there from 1961, leaving about 1970. Eventually the sidings were taken back about 200 yards and a large mound of earth placed across the end of them. I seem to remember some old tools, drills etc being mysteriously thrown into the mess before the insurance people turned up!" Roger Frisby added that carriages coming into the back of the factory happened twice while he worked there. "No-one was ever killed but many were badly shaken. The picture in question was, I think, the accident in 1963."
NBL2085

NBL2086

● This boxy boat was designed to be used either as a caravan or to be slid off its trailer and used as a houseboat, writes Graham Martin. He says: "Northampton Caravans Ltd of Buttocks Booth, were agents for them. I worked for Northampton Caravans at this time and the man in the picture is Mr R. G. Stevens, who was the owner of the company, and the lady in the boat in your other picture was his wife. I believe the stretch of water is Billing Lakes and the photo was probably taken in 1959."

NBL2087

● The mystery of the pensioners apparently off on a coach trip to Moscow has been solved by Phil Wright, who tells us: "The coach was owned by Premier Coaches of Guilsborough and, as a publicity stunt, it travelled from Mansion House, London, to Red Square, Moscow. The coach here is shown picking up at Sywell en route to Clacton, Essex. The coach driver, 10th from the left, is my brother John Wright." Mrs P. Slater says the passengers were Sywell Darby and Joan Club members. The two couples on the right are Mr and Mrs Clayson and Mr and Mrs Clarke. G. Clayson also recognised his parents. Cynthia Rose thought the picture was taken in the 1960s.
NBL2088

● We recognised the Wartburg car and reader Trevor Marks named the owner! He emails: "The picture features Ray Stokes at his home in Warmington, near Oundle. The car was purchased new by him and as far as I know was used to travel daily to Northampton, where he worked, I believe, at Allens, an engineering firm where he was engaged as the works manager. Sadly he passed away about three years ago. His brother Norman was the owner of a motorcycle business in Northampton at that time."
NBL2089

● Retired firefighter Bruce Hoad says this is a Dennis turntable ladder, but that the ladder set has been replaced by some sort of crane. "The chassis design dates back to the mid-1930s and the London Fire Brigade took delivery of the first of these in 1937. As far as I am aware the last batch was delivered to the National Fire Service in 1943."
NBL2090

● Olive Whatton writes: "The car was at Horton Garage, owned by Reginald Sherlock. His wife Margery is standing by the pump attendant, Mrs Thelma Osborne." Mr T. N. Parker added that Mrs Osborne's husband Les also worked at the garage, which was demolished some years ago and is now a small housing estate. Angela Nash also recognised Mrs Sherlock.
NBL2091

● Margaret Ashford (née Matthews) emails: "My father Frank Matthews used to drive this lorry. The photo is not clear enough for me to see if he is driving or is one of the passengers, but we do have a much clearer picture. The steam lorry used to be used as a fundraiser in the carnivals in the county and in Northampton. Dad used to work as an engineer for Phipps Brewery and our home was 151 Bridge Street, Northampton." Wendy Huckerby says the man standing to the left is the brewery's transport manager Bill Lambourne. The Thornycroft lorry, AD 115, is a historic vehicle. It was first registered for road use in 1904. During World War One, it was commandeered for war duties. Phipps Brewery bought it in 1963. It is thought to be the world's oldest surviving steam wagon and is still going strong today.
NBL2092

● Martin Stone tells us the Bedford three-ton lorry was on the parade ground behind the Drill Hall in Clare Street, Northampton. He writes: "Territorial Army soldiers of the Royal Army Service Corps are wearing their polar bear divisional flash. The men are being briefed by their sergeant on the intended route. Convoy work is carefully managed for safety and success. My father was Captain E. J. (Ted) Stone TD of the same unit before it remustered as the Royal Army Ordnance Corps. Both RASC and RAOC were eventually subsumed into the Royal Logistic Corps.
NBL2093

● Aircraft historian Ben Brown, of Sywell Aviation Museum, writes: "You've got a picture of an Aeronca L-16 Champ, taken, judging by the uniforms, in the 1950s or '60s. Interestingly, she has obviously been worked hard as can be seen from the flaking paint on the wing leading edge, and has had a replacement door, which is still in bare metal." Most US bases in the UK had at least one Aeronca Champion for "flying club" usage. Paul Loveday emails: "I would put the picture as possibly late 1950s going by the styles of clothing. The badge on the sleeve jacket is the 8th Army Air Force. Gary Loveday adds: "The guy inspecting the undercarriage is a Senior Airman of the United States Air Force (USAF) and by the numbers on his hat and the badge on his coveralls, he is certainly a member of the 55th Fighter Squadron who were based at Upper Heyford. The other military guy, again USAF, is wearing pilot's clothing which would suggest an officer by the style."

NBL2094

● Ken Lay, a member of the Northampton Section of the Vintage Motor Cycle Club, could not pinpoint the Northampton showroom but he did recognise one of the machines. "I am the owner of the motorcycle in the foreground, registration JNH 996. It is a 1959 model Norton Dominator 88 of 497cc. I purchased the motorcycle privately in January 1979 when it was in a sorry state and hardly recognisable from your photograph. Over a period approaching some 18 months JNH 996, with its original frame, engine and gearbox, was restored by me to its former glory and has since been the recipient of a number of concourse awards. It is hard to put a date on your photograph but judging by the then condition of JNH 996, it looks reasonably new." The motorbikes may have been in the premises of Mick Berrill in Henry Street, Northampton, emails Malcolm Brice. He adds: "The fourth machine, the scooter, looks like a Maicomobil, a fairly rare 200 or 250cc machine, which was the early forerunner of the bigger type of scooter, such as the Yamaha Majesty or Suzuki Burgman sold in the last 15 years."
NBL2095

School's First Days

NBL2096

● Kings Heath Primary School in Northampton was opened by Alderman Cyril Chown on June 23, 1952, and the *Chron's* photographer was there to record the event.

NBL2097

NBL2098

NBL2099

NBL2100

● These pictures show the finishing touches being put to the new building. The school is still going strong and headteacher Jacquie Jackson told us the statue of the boy with the owl is still in place but minus a piece of his arm! She told us in 2006, when we rediscovered these pictures: "The main school building still looks the same but the grass and benches are long gone and we have our nursery unit in that space." She added that the pictures were unearthed at exactly the right time as the school's year five and six children were doing a topic on the 1940s to 1960s.

NBL2101

SHOW TIME

NBL2102

NBL2103

NBL2104

NBL2105

● A glimpse of life more than 50 years ago came to light in a box of dusty glass negatives marked "Timken Show 1955".

The British Timken Show was an institution in Northampton, starting as a garden fête in 1945. It grew and grew until it was bigger than Northampton Balloon Festival is today, with top show-jumping names competing and major attractions such as the Household Cavalry.

In the huge marquees, proud gardeners showed flowers and vegetables with one judge labelling the show "the best in Britain outside Chelsea".

Pets competed for prizes, and it boasted the finest collection of fancy pigeons in Britain and the largest rabbit show in the country. The last show was in 1978. The factory has now gone and the show site earmarked for development.

● Mr W. R. Hughes of Old Duston was able to name some of the people in this picture of the 1955 Timken Show. From left to right are Mr Bennet from the accounts department, the two judges - the one on the right of centre being Britain's best known gardener Percy Thrower - and the gardening shop general foreman Tommy Bannister.
NBL2106

● Another big event in the 1950s and '60s was the County Show, which attracted crowds of up to 15,000. These pictures (left, opposite and on page 74) are from the 1955 show held at Overstone. In later years the show made a loss, and the last one was held in 1971. The Northamptonshire Agricultural Society decided to amalgamate the event with the East of England Show at Peterborough.
NBL2107

NBL2108

NBL2109

YOUNG 'UNS

● These children are from Wappenham School, near Towcester, and were pictured in about 1953, says Robert Keen, who appears on the picture with his brother and sister.
NBL2114

● This is an assembly at Northampton Technical High School, later Trinity School, says Diane Mundin. She was a pupil there during the 1950s and recognised several of her classmates, Gillian Johnson, Avril Hitchcock, Mary Felce, Maureen Harris and Mary Finch. Pauline Thomas spotted herself and several school friends. A dozen old girls from Pauline's time at the school still meet for a meal out every six to eight weeks and are now aged 62 or 63.
NBL2115

● Pam Handley (née Brett) recognised herself playing the finger symbols at Stimpson Avenue School in 1953 and John Hollowell spotted himself playing the drums. Vivienne Murphy (née Willcocks) said she was the conductor and recognised Suzanna York, John Hollowell, Michael King and Kay Johnson. Former teacher D. E. Needle writes: "The children were the 'bulge' just after the war and were about seven years old at this time. I taught the junior department and many of them were in my class in 1954-5. The teacher in the picture was Mrs Jones who lived in Guilsborough. They were the nicest children I taught in 39 years of teaching!"
NBL2116

● Boughton Primary School in 1954 was recognised by Linda Wareing (née Darnell). She is seventh from the right in the back row, next to her best friend Julie Handley. In the centre of the back row are headteacher Mr Wannop and another teacher Miss Nix. David Winter also recognised himself and was able to name teachers Mrs Amey and Mrs Bevis and several pupils. "It was a very happy school," he recalls.
NBL2117

● We guessed correctly when we thought this picture was something to do with our sister paper's children's club, the Mercury Merry Comrades. William Jones says it was taken in 1954 at the Women's Institute building in Litchborough, which is now the village hall. He and his two sisters are on the photograph and he was able to name many more children plus the taller of the adults, Murial Tarry.

NBL2118

● Sheila Brockwell enlisted the help of locals to caption this for us and names the cowboy gang in the bus shelter in Bedford Road, Brafield-on-the-Green as Mick Pittams, Richard Barker and Billy Battison. Mick is now a builder and built the existing bus shelter!

NBL2119

● Stewart Mann writes: "In the Northampton Grammar School photo, I recognise myself, P. V. Maynard and Bill Hooley. I think it was my first year at NGS which would make it 1958 or 1959."
NBL2131

● This church fête in the 1960s was in the grounds of Stone House, home of the Lewis family in New Street, Daventry, writes Celia Sharp. She thinks Tesco now occupies the site. The vicar is the Rev Ward and next to him could be Lady Manningham-Butler.
NBL2132

● Two readers recognised this as the Yardley Hastings Easter Pram Race in 1965. Joan Jeffery emails: "The man pushing the cart with the dog on board is my dad, Bill Underwood. The dog's name was Joe. I think Dad is dressed as Red Riding Hood and the dog is the Wolf in disguise behind the glasses. The annual fancy dress pram race was a great event, bringing the village together no matter what the weather." Diana Heywood adds: "The event was organised by the youth club. The gent in white trousers was Neville Lack (now deceased), and the girl in the pram was Marion King who now lives in Australia."

NBL2133

● Heather Richardson recognised the big dipper at Wicksteed Park, Kettering, and adds: "It doesn't look very big but it was a great ride."

NBL2134

● The fancy dress competition was part of the League of Pity party held at the Salon, Northampton, writes Diana Smith. The three girls "backing Britain" are Kate and Liz Walton and their cousin, Diana's daughter Sue Smith. Diana thinks the year was 1968 and adds: "Thanks for all the old photographs. Having lived in Northampton all my life, I knew one day there must be one I'd recognise!" Heather Richardson (née Earl) writes: "I'm the girl second from left in a pointed hat and my friend Elizabeth Allen is next to me. We went as medieval ladies." She thought the year was 1964.
NBL2135

Kingsley Landmarks

All the landmark buildings the *Chron* pictured in the Kingsley area of Northampton around 1959 have survived to this day.

● St Matthew's Church was built in 1893 by brewery magnate Pickering Phipps as a memorial to his father. It contains several important works of art.
NBL2136

● The Picturedrome, which opened as a cinema in 1912, is now a thriving pub and entertainments venue.
NBL2137

● Kingsley Park Working Men's Club is still going strong.
NBL2138

● The Racecourse Pavilion now houses a restaurant. Horse racing ceased in 1904 after several serious accidents and the area is now a park and venue of the nationally famous Northampton Balloon Festival.
NBL2139

● The White Elephant pub, which overlooks the Racecourse, underwent a change of name in the 1990s but it changed back due to popular demand. NBL2140

SCENES

NBL2141

NBL2142

● Two views of construction work to build the roundabout and approach roads in St Peter's Way, Northampton, in the late 1960s or early '70s. The area of Gas Street is flattened, but we can make out The Gasometer pub and Mr Benn the Barber. The second picture shows the roundabout construction well under way.

● This area of St James, Northampton, is virtually unaltered since this picture was taken in the 1960s. It shows the St James Road junction with Sharman Road. Church's shoe factory is on the left and Northampton Corporation Transport offices are on the right.
NBL2143

● This picture caused some confusion, not least because we used it back to front! We corrected that mistake, and John Lovell tells us it is Northampton Racecourse before 1950. What we thought were marquees were huts erected for a wartime army camp. John Denton also identified the Racecourse. A. D. Hiam reckons the huts were for a prisoner-of-war encampment built during the 1940s on the football and cricket pitches. Once the war ended, many of the Italian POWs moved to Bedford to work in brick-making.
NBL2144

● This picture of the bottom of Bridge Street, Northampton, brought back memories for Paul Wilkins, who writes: "The large white van is parked outside the Eastern Electricity Board offices. The Bull and Butcher pub and a fish and chip shop owned by Mr J. Edmunds were located beyond the Ford Popular.
NBL2145

● Colin Wooding was an apprentice at Robert A. Baldwin's Clock Shop in Kettering Road, Northampton, from 1950 to 1956, when this picture was taken. He writes: "I then did my National Service, rejoined Robert in 1958, and became his partner in the 1970s when we changed the name to Baldwin and Wooding, The Watch Workshop. I worked on the premises from leaving school until I was 65 and closed the shop in 2000." Harvey Fisher emailed: "Bob Baldwin was a member of the Northampton Society of Model Engineers. He built a three-and-a-half inch gauge locomotive, named Midgett, which was an 0-6-0 side tank locomotive, which he ran on the Delapre Park track. He also loaned the locomotive out to members of the club. The track is still in use today."
NBL2146

● Mr R. G. Streeter used to work at Grose's in Marefair, Northampton, and later returned to the area to work for Barclaycard, which was built on the same site. Dominic Bodily reckons the picture was taken in the late 1960s, as the Barclaycard offices were constructed around 1968.
NBL2147

● Ron Johnson was interested in this photo of Kettering Road and emails: "I used to be taken there to have my hair cut in the late 1950s. You had to walk through the front shop first which was an angler's paradise, and in the back was the barber's shop. I can smell the hair oils and embrocations to this day! I think the same man ran both shops." Mrs W. Barker and David Blackburn also had fond memories of this area and Colin Wilkins emails: "The barber's behind the fishing tackle shop was my father's business and before that my grandfather's. The shop was A. T. Wilkins and continued after father's death in 1956 under the proprietorship of Frank Tite, until it was demolished in the mid-1970s. Frank Tite continued to run a barber's shop in premises opposite for some years after this. Originally the hairdressing and fishing tackle were in separate shops, the hairdressing situated in Kettering Road opposite Henry Street. Around 1953, Father combined the two by adding a salon to the back of the shop where the Mini is in the photo."
NBL2148

NBL2149

● "Your photograph of Steve Clarke & Sons' spring window display is of the shop that used to be in Kettering Road, just above Clare Street," writes Valerie Baker. "The two ladies are Mrs Hilda Garwood on the right, and me, then Miss Perrin, some 50 years ago, both employed as sales assistants. On that particular day we were posing as customers for the benefit of a promotional photograph. Happy, happy days, thanks for the memory."

● Another of Steve Clarke's shops was in Abington Street, Northampton. Jackie Atkins says her mother worked there in the 1960s. These shops were near the top of Abington Street and were opposite the Wedgwood Cafe, emailed Dawn Bonham. Donald Ball worked in the Phillips menswear shop from its opening in 1956, when the firm came down from Lewisham. Next to Phillips was the Gayeway School of Dancing, he recalls, and the entrance is still there. Barrie Clarke remembers the photograph being taken from the first floor of the Wedgwood Cafe opposite. He emails: "The store had just moved across the road and I am standing by the car on the right of the picture, having just moved it from in front of the shop to allow the photographer a clear view of the modern facade! Steve Clarke's was a Northampton family business of which I was a director, and at the height of its business had 24 shops around the Midlands, including five in Northampton. I believe this photograph was taken in the mid-1960s." Mrs C. Lovell added: "I was one of the assistants at Steve Clarke's who sold affordable shoes." And finally, Judith Bird writes: "My father Spencer Clarke owned the shop along with many others in the town and county. My husband Anthony Bird came into the business in 1961 and my cousin Barrie was also involved. The Maltese manager of the shop, Charles Scerri, is also in the photograph standing between the two cars on the left."

NBL2150

● "Rayboulds used to belong to the parents of my Uncle John," writes Wendy Collier. "Auntie June and my mum used to do all the alterations for the customers." Rayboulds was in Kettering Road, Northampton. NBL2151

● "I am the young lady in the poppy seller photograph," writes Annette Sharp. "I am with my young brother, Clive Warren and my daughter Amanda is in the pushchair. This must have been taken in November 1966. It was great to see the chrome mudguards on the pushchair!" The poppy seller is outside Northampton Guildhall. NBL2152

● Marks & Spencer's new store in Abington Street, Northampton, is being built. The store opened in late 1969.
NBL2153

● R. Canning, Ray Whiting and Paul Wilkins all write to say the flatbed lorry is struggling up a snowy London Road, Northampton, with the Abbey on the left. Mr Whiting reckons it was the winter of 1962-3, when he could not work for three months due to such bad weather.
NBL2154

● The picture of Cherry Orchard School, Northampton, was taken in the mid-1960s, emails Phil Boswell. "The bubble car belonged to geography teacher Doug Betts. I think the two teachers on the edge of the path in the middle distance are Derek Brooks (careers) and Mr Murphy (games). The three cherry trees on the grass area were planted by fifth year leavers after they had finished their GCE O-levels. My year planted ours in 1971. It was one of the school traditions. I went back to the school in the 1990s as a supply teacher when it had become a mixed middle school. Two teachers from my time as a pupil, Mr Howland and Mr Martin, were still teaching there then. It was a strange experience to go from former pupil to colleague!" Brian Whitworth remembered the bubble car was blue. Andrew Hiam reckons the picture was taken in early September 1969, and he may be one of the boys in it.
NBL2155

● Our picture of the now-demolished St Andrew's Church, Semilong, Northampton, brought back memories for Margaret Haycock. She writes: "I used to live facing St Andrew's when I was small. It was called Bell Barn Street. I also got married there on March 29, 1952."
NBL2156

● The picture of an elderly couple walking past a demolition site in Northampton stirred memories for several readers. Helen O'Callaghan emails: "This picture is a view of Mount Gardens looking from the Mounts towards Lady's Lane. The house at the end with the white windows is where my grandparents lived for a time in the 1930s. My grandfather was a fireman based at the newly-opened Mounts Fire Station... so very handy for work! They lived in Mounts Gardens as my grandmother refused to live in the flats above the station because she had a young family (with heavy prams) and there was no lift. My dad tells me that the building next door belonged to Underwood and Weston the builders, and the roof which can be seen over the house is Randalls Shoe Factory." Former Mount Gardens resident Linda Hillery (née Hall) writes: "This cut-through is between The Mounts and Lady's Lane. We lived there around 1955." Dave Collins adds: "The houses in the right-hand picture are the rear of the houses on The Mounts, where the court buildings are now. The house to the right of the tree, with the three windows, is where my grandparents' (Mr & Mrs Sidney Collins) newsagent shop was. Rod Sharp emails: "It was a paved area with houses on each side and it linked the Mounts to Lady's Lane. As children it was a short cut we used to take from the Mount Baths to the town centre. Happy days." Finally Frank Jeffs emails: "Mount Gardens ran from The Mounts roughly opposite the Swimming Baths to Lady's Lane. It was still there in the 1950s."
NBL2157

● This is a fête in the garden of Holcot Rectory in the early '60s, emails Jo Moulds. "I am almost sure the lady was the person who had opened the fête. The gentleman in charge of the croquet game was George Gurney who was the verger for 37 years." The car in the background is a Triumph Herald coupé.

NBL2158

● This interesting building was identified by Ian
Stephens as Holly Lodge. He adds: "It can be seen
when travelling between Boughton and Moulton.
It is part of an interesting group of buildings
(including a folly) associated with Boughton House."
NBL2159

● The man with the Alsatians has been identified as Cyril Mathison by the reporter who wrote the story, back in 1953! John Morris said: "The story that went with this picture was written by myself and appeared in the *Northampton Independent*, then a weekly magazine. I have a cutting of the story and picture in my very first scrapbook after joining the *Chron* as a reporter in August 1953. The Northamptonshire Alsatian Circle had just been formed and had recently won its first awards at the Northampton Canine Society show." Dominic Bodily thought the picture was taken at the Ex-Service Working Men's Club in Sheep Street, Northampton.

NBL2171

● This family gathering was to celebrate the 100th birthday of Mrs E. Poole, of Church Lane, Bugbrooke, says her grandson John Billingham. From left are Gordon Barnes and his wife Pam, John's mother Nina, his grandmother, his aunts Catherine Meaning and Lottee, his sister Barbara and Henry Barnes. He adds: "Grandma broke her hip at 100 years of age and lived to be 102 (1863-1965). She died at her daughter Catherine's home in the Isle of Wight. I was pleased to see the photo and roll back the years." Readers Jane Barker and Pam Frost also recalled the occasion. Jane remembers children from the village school taking gifts to Mrs Poole. "Granny" Poole was Pam's grandfather's next-door neighbour.

NBL2172

● This shows Northampton Jewish ex-servicemen who were going to London for their annual Remembrance Parade, which was held the week after the national one, says Mrs G. Pollock. She thinks it was taken in the early 1950s and the gentleman in the centre is her father, Morris Jaffa, who owned Roses curtain shop in Abington Street and was for many years chairman of the Poppy Appeal. Holding the standard is Len Burman, and the man on the left, front row, without a hat, is a Mr Black who was a hairdresser near the Guildhall. Next to him is Sid Cipin, who with his brother, Myer, owned Northampton cinemas, including the Plaza in Wellingborough Road. The tallest man in the centre of the second row is Frank Gale, who owned Florella Modes in Gold Street.

NBL2173

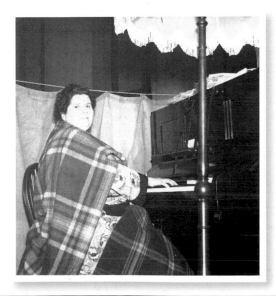

● The pianist is Musical Marie, playing at the old skating rink at the top of Abington Street, Northampton, in the 1950s, say Mrs K. Harrison, Ray Whiting, Maureen Cook and Roy Mallard. She played the piano for about five days. Mrs P. Slater thinks that Marie was trying to break the world record but can't remember if she achieved her aim. Mrs Slater called in to watch at least three times on her way to work. An internet search revealed that Marie Ashton of Stretford reached her goal of breaking the world record for continuous piano in Queen Street Assembly Rooms, Rawtenstall, Lancashire, in May 1954. She completed her 132-hour marathon with the national anthem, after which her hands had to be lifted from the keys.

NBL2174

● The story behind this broken fireplace was more dramatic than we could have imagined! June Davis (née Watts) recognised herself in 1952 aged 19 with her bedroom grate. She writes: "A thunderbolt had come down the chimney in the early hours and blew the whole grate out. At the time I lived in Semilong Road, Northampton. It brought back a lot of memories for me."
NBL2175

● This was taken outside Towcester Town Hall, probably at the 1966 General Election when Northamptonshire South was won by Conservative Arthur Jones, writes Anthony Ward. He adds: "In the middle is Sir Reginald Manningham-Butler (later Lord Dilhorne). His daughter, Eliza, recently retired as head of MI6."
NBL2176

● Lots of readers wrote to tell us about Sabrina opening the Victor Value supermarket in Abington Street, Northampton, in 1957. Barry Andrews says: "She opened what was purported to be Northampton's first supermarket. I was in my early teens and among the crowd outside, which was so thickly packed together that I was able to lift my feet off the floor and be carried along. Sabrina was portrayed on TV as a dumb blonde. Dumb in so far as I don't ever recall her saying anything when she appeared on TV." Derek King recalls that Sabrina was discovered by Arthur Askey and adds that Sabrina was the name of the goddess of the River Severn. Keith Andrews agreed that Sabrina did and said nothing! "Her only asset was that she possessed a large bust. It was in the 42-44 inch bracket... quite a sight in the 1960s." John Franks adds more details: "Her real name was Norma Ann Sykes. She had blonde hair, blue eyes and a 42-23-36 figure. She appeared with Arthur Askey and had cameo roles in a few films and theatre work." Anthony Ward reckons Sabrina was one of the first so-called celebrities. He agrees Victor Value was the first supermarket in Northampton.
NBL2177

● Julie Shaw (née Sykes) emails: "This was a spring fayre at the Central Methodist Church when it was on Regent Square, Northampton, where the Gala Casino is now. I am the girl presenting a gift to the gentleman, and my dark-haired friend beside me is Kathleen Sample. The lady receiving a gift is Ruby Murray who opened the fayre and the gentleman is her husband. I believe the boy in the picture is Martin Pettit." Heather Davies (née Lansbury) kindly sent us a copy of the church magazine which reported on the success of the Dutch Spring Fayre, held on March 22, 1969, and raised £463. She writes: "The people in the photo are Minister of the church, the Rev G. Clifford Hunt, chairman of the fayre Arthur Jolley, and singer, stage and TV star Ruby Murray. All of our parents were members of the Central Methodist Church, and then Kingsthorpe Methodist Church and it was a big part of our childhood and is still part of our lives." Singer Ruby Murray lived in Northamptonshire and often went out of her way to help local charities, including the *Mercury & Herald* Merry Comrades. Her name lives on as Cockney rhyming slang for curry.
NBL2182

● "These dogs belonged to Northants Dog Training Club," writes Jean Dolman. "We owned the collie (second from right), Jenny. The photograph would have been taken in the early 1960s, but I cannot be sure where. The club is still going strong after 51 years and my husband and I are joint presidents." Andrew Hiam says this is Great Billing Fayre in June or July 1966-7. He writes: "The left hand tent was used by both the Scouts and Boys' Brigade units for camping. The middle tent could sleep 12 Scouts quite easily. The right hand tent was normally hired out by the borough council for larger events in the town and British Timken shows."
NBL2183

● This is the Blisworth Merry Comrades May Festival in 1955, writes Jean Cadd. The Merry Comrades was a children's group run by the *Northampton Mercury & Herald* newspaper and which raised money for good causes. In charge of them was "Auntie Dick" – Mrs Bernice Field – who is crowning the May Queen, Mrs Cadd's younger sister, Ann Perkins. Mrs Cadd thinks two of the other girls are Sally Holding and Rita Stewart. Frank Holding, who worked for E. M. Rogers of Duston, drove the lorry. Jackie Parish also recognised Auntie Dick.

NBL2184

● Another Merry Comrades May Queen, this time outside Sywell Church. Mrs P. Slater writes: "Margaret Mabbutt is being crowned by, I believe, Kathleen Gurney. To mention a few of the girls, they are Pauline and Wendy Sweetingham, Hilary Osborne, Deborah Reeve and Susan Rose."

NBL2185

● Brian Paling emails: "The fête was held at Flore House in the late 1950s. Ron Forge (who still lives in the village) is on the right." The lad in the background is Jim Stone, writes his cousin Celia Sharp. "The object of this game was to see how many pegs one could take off the line without dropping them."

NBL2186